TYPICAL TRAGEDIES:
A BOOK OF POETRY

By Patrick Ashe

ISBN: 978-1-7348477-3-4

Cover Design: James Kenyon
Formatting: C&D Editing

With special gratitude to Mom, Dad (In Memoriam), Dr. Hollis Earl Pruitt (In Memoriam), Shelley, Mrs. Murray, my classmates and all who encouraged me to keep writing.

Table of Contents

I: HERE, HEAR

HEAR THE FIGHT HERE

Hear the sound of the Truth
In the stuttering of forced feat
The feckless tries and holy cries
Of failure propped on honored seat

Here is the Unreal seen
In aging haze and doubting clout
It reaches through what we all knew
Was real enough to keep us out

Hear the songs of Cursed Voice
Sung so discordant that it bleeds
For we wanted to be hunted
By the ends of our own deeds

Here is the Blessed Hand
Forging the hammer to judge right
Of my own life and our shared strife
Now is the time to fight. Fight. FIGHT.

DO I STILL HAVE IT?

Do I still have it?
Or should I fold my hand and leave?
Do I still have it?
Is there a mace up my sleeve?

When you've lost the First World battles
And you're kicking back in Passchendaele
The rains of rejection falling harder still
Making the muck as soft as a mourning veil

In this trench of screens and missed connection
Or a rudderless boat seeking direction
From a sky the color of a deep infection
Glad to still float with holes in each section

So I gotta lotta nerve to flag you down
And throw one more heart on the unlit pyre
Because at least one will be pulled
Then the rest will burn ever higher

Of course, this isn't all there is
Despite every other message than this
Try your hand and don't you quit
Even if I don't still have it

. . .

Or I do

Fuck if I know anymore

THE DAY THAT SHE REMARRIED

The day that she remarried
I had laid upon my face
A dozen roses of torn skin
A reason for disgrace

The day that she remarried
I didn't click on them
The pictures of the cruise, her man,
Her dress from stern to hem

The day that she remarried
I was not so much bereft
Nor even caring we never married
Just that anything was left

The day that she remarried
I was married, too
But how can one be truly wed
To anyone but you

The day that she remarried
I didn't send my best
You don't even want it so
Please enjoy the rest

EGO-ALTER

You said you wanted Superman
I gave you Clark Kent

You declined, turned off by

The way my arm gets caught

Taking off the suit

THIS OLD CAR

I'm still driving this old thing
It's an '82 something or other
Usually other
American made piece of work

Ran pretty well for ten years
Not many miles, just a bad collision
Really bad
Never drove the same after that

I was in denial for awhile
Didn't want to take it into the shop
Finally did
Apparently it was extremely overdue

What exactly was wrong
It was a bit of everything
Under the hood
But the dents in the doors were my fault

I got it running for awhile
Made it to school and work
I mean
It only broke down on my time

So I still maintain it

It's all I can afford

But sometimes

I still kick the doors because it kind of sucks

HOOKS AND CHAINS OF MIND

I am not defined by my hooks and chains of mind
I am not defined by them but they are with me all the time

I wanted to enjoy a conversation with a friend
I wanted to enjoy it but the hooks pulled at me again

I wanted to be productive on all the tasks around
I wanted to be productive but on a chain I'm bound

I am not defined by my hooks and chains of mind
I am not defined by them but they keep me from my kind

I swore again that I would reach across that finish line
I swore again I'd do it but by my foot I am entwined

I swore again that I could do a simple little thing
I swore again I'd do it but a hooked mouth cannot sing

I am not defined by my hooks and chains of mind
I am not defined by them but I'm the one I must remind

BABY, LIGHT MINE FIRE

I know now what happens
With the unstoppable force and the immovable object
I learn it every day and forget it again
Until I rant to some poor ear like yours
Hear the tale of the Centralia, Pennsylvania Mine Fire.

There is a town up there, off Highway 81 revisited
Under which the coal steam fire burns for decades since
And decades to come, until it will die
Exactly like my passion, it keeps burning intensely and throughout

It doesn't stop
And has nowhere to go

This flame is for internal use only

As curious as this event may be, and less for how it concerns me
Whether a cautionary tale about coal steam treatment
Or another keen simile or metaphor for me to steal
Perhaps the most important takeaway from it all
Is that Centralia, Pennsylvania
Was all but abandoned long ago.

Won't you be mine neighbor?

MAUDLIN AGENCY

There is no more poisoned well

No more wounded gazelle

No bluer bruise

No older shoes

No drier lip

No wetter ship

No bloodier pulp

No greater gulp

No smaller hope

No tighter rope

No grayer plant

No greater defeat of can by can't

Than my ego

WHISTLING IN THE DARK BY THEY MIGHT BE GIANTS

It was a song I heard then
From days of innocence
But now it's just a symbol
Of what I've become since

For what is surely giant
Is dark that is manmade
You can call me a liar
I'll call a shade a shade

I know I have no excuse
For bitchings in my rap
Like sprinkles in your ice cream
They'll both turn into crap

But you, too, should be grateful
For sore eyes in the light
Which comes from someone greater
Than the day or the night

Does it matter if I'm glum
When in the dark I sing
For there is where I still hear
The few bells that still ring

CALL AND RESPONSE

When the world says
Go away
We don't want you here

One should respond
Too bad
Take it up with who sent me

II: BAD HIGH SCHOOL POETRY

BAD HIGH SCHOOL POETRY

This is bad high school poetry
That is bad high school poetry
But this puts the ass in alliterative assonance
With crap the consistency of caramel
Written in bad high school calligraphy

This is a decent grade school critique
And a downright good preschool stink
Where cunning repetition and coprophilic references are
considered rectitude

Congrats

From diaper to diploma

But yours still stinks

THE YOUNG NIGHTMARE

Love LOVE
Suck it sensually, not too sensually
Not too sweet
You know it is a butterfly wing waiting to collapse
If it is caressed by the wrong creature

So if I lay my life down by the sewage of hell
Perhaps I can buy my way back into heaven
Only lustful passion is left anyway
Here come the day's curtains
My eyes come to a close

End death overkill
A hurricane triggered by butterfly wings
A flattening nuclear holocaust some x times the size of hiroshima
How fitting, auschwitz and cherry pits and her sweet lips
Have something in common . . . and so . . .

You roll me over, preheat to 450
I'll grab the scalpel, you can sit still
Today in our biochemistry of relationships class we will study . . .
. . . confidence evaporation
Open your hands, close your eyes
Here comes the surprise

But I cannot, as I would rather consume this pyre

Than leave what is about a .01% chance of being . . .

. . . Salvation

But being a typical tragedy, it sank in its maiden glory

Right after leaving the dock

Then there was a void

Like something in dante's inferno past circle seven

But if you read it like professor what's his name told you to

You would know that there is more in hell

But my conscience told this unto me

Part of you must be destroyed

To ransom the self-inflicted hemorrhage of your brethren

And withstand until the heart comes before the eclipse

Only then can you make that tired old request

To be taken home

Home to what?

Love?

NOW THAT YOU'RE DEAD, DEAR SAILOR

Now that you're dead, dear sailor
And freed by the vast omniscient sea
One such infinitesimal factual jetsam you now possess
Is any such greatness that I quite presumably possess

As my humility melts upon the thought
I have stopped to notice
That it may be, just may be
Comparable to the greatness
Of you
Under red skies

But also a shitton of other people

Sail on, sail on, sail on.

I WANNA BE LIKE LEONARD

It should be obvious by now
That I'm not above hero worship
And prone to riffing therein
And just conceited enough to spin a track right now

Oh, if I could be like Leonard
So I can speak intimately with strangers
About the distances of lovers
And make a name for myself by 40

I was told I was born old
An Altar Boy Scout who would be Priest, Prophet, and King
Certainly the best kid at make-believe
Starting a lifelong love affair with Death on memento mori stickies

Then came the mighty ledger
Of loss, inadequacy, heartbreak, insecurity, rejection, illness, failure,
indolence, guilt, indulgence, defeat, irritability, disillusionment,
ineptitude, ennui, ire, and worst of all . . .
Awkwardness
They number like wine receipts for Leonard and me

But he was the sighing Rumpelstiltskin of song and pen
Spinning those last straws into gold
And I am just an old spinning wheel
Whining for a little grease

20

WHEN LOVERS MEET

A lover met many people. One of these was special. But this one thought the lover was too x. The lover wept and continued.

The lover met many more people. One of these was special. But that one thought the lover was not x enough. The lover wept and continued.

The lover met many more people. One of these was special. But that one thought the lover wasn't a lover. The lover wept and continued.

The lover met many more people. One of these was special. But that one thought the lover shouldn't be a lover. The lover wept and continued.

A long time later, the lover met someone very special. This one loved the lover. But the lover learned that they were both long dead.

finis

I'M NOT A LOSER I'M NOT A LOSER I'M NOT A LOSER

There are no winners
There are no losers
There is only potential in varying degrees of fulfillment

There are no winners
There are no losers
But Sean Connery said in that movie I'm just whining about best
and won't get to go home and

There are no winners
There are no losers
Would a loser keep using the same old hackneyed devices to write
that

There are no winners
There are no losers
Would a winner bother to be reading this

There are no points to obsessing about who is who
Just do your best and go home before any dumb writer fills your
head with platitudes
That don't really fit anyone's experiences

Sean's the best at Celebrity Jeopardy, though

DUPLI-CITY

Here's to the inescapable
The annually obligatory
Tracing my roots on the road of time to
Anxious ambivalence as a place

Where the sun is always shining
From deep golden glass
Over green hills, gray streets, orange stuff
And with tension as rays

It is truly a land of plenty
Plenty of judgments over nothing
And arguments over nothing
Yet many quiet mournings, too

I don't mean to speak ill
It would be self-defeating anyway
But you have to call a spade a spade
When it awaits your side on entry

I just wish it was better
Like I wish I was better
Still the road comes back around
Here's to the inescapable

THE TRUE BALLAD OF DUDLEY STARLUST

He came from Tennessee, Dudley Starlust wanted to be
On all the screens, so that all his friends would see
He'd practice the strut and play basic riffs but now
He was bound and determined to break out of his hometown

The best way he could see was that ol' eMpTy Vee
Contacts promised him a spot on thirty silver screens
All that this required was turning people into things
Mixing means with the ends, but the brass wear all the rings

Pushing from beneath of his sordid little fad
Was the sordid support of an evil, evil dad
Why shouldn't others suffer a bit like Dudley did
Magnanimity made no hit from even a skilled kid

Dudley wailed upon their heads as he headed westward bound
A guitar in his hand, but no crossroads would be found
Ready and willing to cut himself the Devil's deal
Even the Devil didn't want a soul like his to steal

It's sad but it's true that Dudley's only highs were from meth
Despite all the better bandmates he had threatened with a death
Until one day, they say, he did strike a man down, you see
It only saddens me for all . . . though I'm surprised it wasn't me

SERIOUS THINGS

If I told you
Serious things
You would not believe me

I know this because

I already have

And you still don't

UNFRIENDING RAMPAGE

You put the end in friend, so I sought to end one-way friendships.

I started with social media, of course. Deleted the hell out of those sleazy sorts.

Then went the fair-weather farewells. I miss those select spells, but oh well.

And social groups? We all know they were never friends to lose.

It got a little tough with some long-timers. But we've grown into other timelines.

Finally came the close ones. This is where they find disclosure.

Eventually, there weren't many people left.

Any.

Whatever.

My dog came with me to my cat's grave. We had a good day.

ONTOLOGICAL EVIL

I don't have to believe in the Devil
I know he exists
As well as anyone can
Certainly more than you

The evidence is abundant
He's a sound in my head
He's the pinnacle of absurdity
He's my most obsessive fan
Leaning into the rail to watch me decorate the tracks with my
shattering pieces

He's always there
He's always there
He's always there
He's always there
He's always there
He's always there
He's always there
He's always there
He's always there
He's always there
He's always there
He's always there
He's always there

III: SEE, I CAN WRITE ABOUT POSITIVE THINGS

SEE, I CAN WRITE ABOUT POSITIVE THINGS

Converse on toeses and laps full of kittens
Cheap but nice tube amps all ripe for my rippins
Customized Ibanez strung with six strings
See, I can write about positive things

Dream-flooded REM sleep and flying all lucid
Warm beds and trailheads and your thoughts unmuted
Threadbare sport t-shirts from long ago springs
See, I can write about positive things

Swimming within a blue wave as it crashes
Day ends and good friends joining in the splashes
Trembles in voices as we exchange rings
See, I can write about positive things

When the part comes with the bad stuff
Then I'm super glad
I could go wild with my negative things
But miss my chance – now I'm sad

HOW MUSIC IS MADE

Music is made in the intervals
The spaces between the notes
And the rhythm with which each are played
Mostly where differences are told

Common time and common structures
Are much like water or a walk
Four is for what comes naturally to most
Unfolding like tapestries or growing like mold

There is no virtue in trying to be
Purposefully different nor the same
Like dark and light and hot and cold
The interplay is where they come into play

One must start with a sense or two
Of relationships between these marks
Unraveling an honest expression
Responding to what inspiration may say

So try to check one's vanity
In hopes of vision tapping into reality
Value for others comes with loss of certainty
That sounds will resonate eternally

LIGHTNING IN MY HANDS

When from that beautiful bend over nickel string by steel fret
ringing pinch harmonic major wailing trill on whammy bar with
heavy sand pick hand right strike vibrating deep into sweet ceramic
pickup set within breathtaking blue popular burl atop African
mahogany plunging through premium wire cable circuitry
numerous knobs in perfect pedal board overdrive on through
chiming chorus delay one delay two reverberation resonating
preamp power amp EL84 vacuum tube speaking speaker cable
speakers sing gloriously through my room at all hours of the night
with just the right TONE TONE TONE TONE to my highly
subjective ear at the moment THE MOMENT THE MOMENT AHH
SING SING YOU GLORIOUS TOOLS SING FOR ME

I feel lightning

Lightning in my hands

SNOW DOG

When last of the big fat flakes
Fall across these hills of snow
I lace my boots and call my dog
For adventure we will go

Into the trees so dark and tall
Into the land so pure
Into the winds of peaceful glens
Into my soul, a cure

And once we have found a spot
To rest and to proclaim
The wondrous and solemnity here
Knowing courage and no shame

I call to my dog and hear her run
Her huffing and feet so quick
We carry back to the same old
With a little more kick for it

THOUGH I RETURN TO HOMELAND, LORD

Though I return to homeland, Lord
My zeal is met with dread
As grateful I am it remains homeland
I pray it so when I am dead.

For nary a craft I find myself
In spite of good preparation
So be it, Lord, if You see fit
For a higher kept expectation.

Still the abundance of the ire in me
I humbly pray You doth forgive
It is but spoil from love of this land
That my old family did live.

So I try now to love it still
As the new river that it be
Prudence holds what Providence knows
That forward is how we see.

Keep to my heart as I look out
O'er this good land and sky
And be with all its good people, Lord
Wherever I am to die.

SUSPICIOUSLY SPECIFIC

My legs were not cut
I still feel them there
My legs were not cut
All there everywhere

My legs were not cut
By those saying kneel
But if they were right
I guess I must heal

IV: UNFINISHED SONGS

THE WORST OF THIS WORLD

Misshapen piece meets the wolven white world
Merit lost to the plutocratic cost
Might makes right, unnatural law might
Help me to put the utility in the futility

It's a misconception beyond all perception
I'm an ideal type without breath, sickness unto death
If I let my guard down, you just keep hitting
And take all your shit, you just keep shitting

I am the worst of this world – I am the worst of your world

Kept kicking this machine programmed for defeat
Wondered why it didn't work, set "beat" on repeat
I'm a jack-shit of all trades, master of no fun
Try-fail ratio steep, bleeding under feet

But whose standards are truly lower
When I want truth and you need lies
I've lost all the battles, will I win the war
May this be the bunker, I can see your eyes

I am the worst of this world – I am the worst of your world
I am nothing to all of you, but am I something to . . .

TO SOLVE YOUR PROBLEMS

Obfuscate the solution, the problem pulls behind
Obfuscate the problem, and the solution pulls further

My weak wall fell, I just need a lift
Just one chance, just a little lift
I'll give fifty . . . hundred, ten grand, for a lift
I'll give a rotten old soul for a lift

Solve my problems, crush a dribbled brain
Give me a god, prison securely gained
Solve my problems, death train of the heart
Give me a god, the conscience must rot

Benefactor and hater, give me a god
No sex now, but later you'll be a god
It's that problem, I swear please GOD
It's all your fault I think GOD

So now he's mine, the spherical knife
Solvent of pain, solvent of life
Solution to all, and all but sin
Left to corrode all the feelings within

Spitter-spat small drain for surging serotonin all up in the synaptic
cleft from a 200mgs sucky-sucky of partyoxetine hydrochloride
wait now I know or was that the big god or was that Him or I don't

39

know but it was bubble heartburn vomit (hack, gag) just a side effect
but wait, there's the brain pick it a bit or no no no not that that's just
so GOD

Where's God?
Give me my damn SSRIs
Where's God?
Give me my damn lithium
Where's God?
Give me my damn SNRIs
Where's God?
Give me my damn MAOIs

Oh, there He i —

ACCEDE TO MY UNDERTOW

So it's figured out now
For the search, where's the truth? Here it comes
Then it's done, a gang-bang explanation
The smug one takes a bow, the charmed one takes a bow

And his mind spilled right out
Revealed the dark tempest once called intent
Conscience feeling errant, it's all quite apparent
Truth is a club, and now I'm allowed

Try to atone for the empty sphere in here
Die all alone, serene fear so near (it speaks)

"I hate all that you would know
Accede to my undertow
So unassured, let it grow
Accede to my undertow"

Life gapes open, negation looming
Lucifer tears your soul straight out of your
Chest caving in, you know nothing's within
Except that superfluous shit consuming

My senses on lock and my drive a cage
Blood pumping harder, colder, faster to
Affirm the feed, please surrender the need

Love is a drink, and I'm not of age

Slipped in, fell in
It's all my sin
If I only knew
Or had a clue
Not figured out now
He wouldn't allow
Not figured out yet
And I cannot forget
So continuing on . . .

THE RECESSES OF EXCESSES

We're full of passion, emptied of thought
Yin with the sin implodes a sentimental drought
Fantasy elation, emotional masturbation
Fulfilling what the mind of the body has sought

Always for love, never for Love left
Divine gamble yields one or a death
Like sand in a sore, my heart is a whore
Far past our need we take a deep breath

Man and woman, Adam and Eve
We are with them and we will never leave
Forever the scorn, nothing is born
Hearts stay torn with no one to grieve

The other two are drugs and barely elate
I've spent half of my life doing what I hate
And spent the other fucking up what I love
Our descent into half-hugs is a twist of fate

Glimmered hope locked in a box so small
I overturned the table and took out the shelves
Found an evolutionary flaw embedded in us all
And this is what we made of ourselves

HUMAN MACHINE

And he thought he could think for himself
Without compromising mental health
He thought he could live, thought he could love
Without punishment from all above

Inch by inch, his soul will deplete
Faith full of thought is so obsolete
Come to the slaughter, such a pity
To reject our machine, so violently pretty

Get in line, he who does not understand
We have a solution for you and the band
Feed the machine until gears gleam in blood
We take your life and we get a red flood

I've said it once, I've said it a billion times - send 'em down the hall
Crush 'em, kill 'em, send 'em, no one
Burn 'em, fuck 'em, drop 'em, no one
No one shall ever oppose our machine

Human, human machine
Question your vanity, question your sanity
Human, human machine
Question if you're truly free

TERMINAL FUN

The modern man, his societal lie
"God's man kills, so why can't I?"
Little stimulation, a quiet little death
Half gram of soma on a bated breath

C-drive, cell, and terminal fun
Daily grinder is number one
A soul is to sell, my sedentary son
Daily grinder is terminal fun

Arrogance expands as a soul contracts
The passion of pride conflicts with facts
Conformity lust in everyone's eyes
A rebellion farce, the true self dies

To everything – burn, burn, burn!
This is our season to burn, burn, burn!
To everything – burn, burn, burn!
This is our season to burn, burn, burn middle suburbia.

Mr. Polo Shirt I meet in a walk
Emptying my mind over our small talk
I tell him to open his Book, and then he will see
To be the world's friend is to be God's enemy

I AIM TO BLEED

Shall I fall before your almighty brilliance?
Or blame myself for lackluster vigilance?
Suffice to say, I can only aim to seethe
When I've done everything right, but I forgot to breathe

Aim, your primary target's here
To what end, your subtle hate and fear?
Bleed me dry, but it's all clear
Why do I aim to bleed?

Prevarication, vilification, alienation
Falls from an invisible face
Hypocrisy has its way
While we, the few, burn in place

Aim, your primary target's here
To what end, your subtle hate and fear?
Bleed me dry, but it's all clear
Why must I aim to bleed?

All succumb to this impervious project of sin
Some will kill their hearts and their children
In the postmodern world, the ego is in
We're all spotted, clotted, and rotted with sin

V: STICKING IT TO DEMAND

ENTRY

It's a door closed on an already mangled foot

A toilet for blood, sweat, and tears

Pissing away time

A vessel stuck under its rescuers

Unsolicited advice

Missing all the shots taken

Shooting for the moon and landing among the scars

Kindly worded rejection notices

Unsent rejection notices

Stress for its own sake

The death knell of meritocracy

A mockery of division of labor

Knock, knock, knocking on Kafka's door

A coin always coming up tails

Resenting the notion of luck

Hours of paperwork never read

Lessened duration of delayed gratification

Having no excuse

Having nothing to lose and still losing

Taking the road less traveled by and breaking both ankles

It's a really bad way to spend your waning breaths

It's not entry

CONSOLATION PRIZES

Don't cry for me, Suburban America
For I've been awarded many consolation prizes
And they're not just for participation

Perspective
Enough red ink
Good taste in music
Having children late in life
Spikes in cortisol when hearing from you
Putting the certainty in uncertainty
Acute awareness of my flaws
Lowered expectations
Petty desires
Character
Your rot

I can't wait to show you the trophy case
It ties the tenement together nicely
But you don't visit anymore

THE CLAUSE OF THE WORLD (DEVOUR WITHIN)

The ones who want to serve
Are so easily manipulated by those who serve and are served
Those with a place, from the greatest halls to the thinnest walls
Their elusive approval asks for anything and everything, leaving
An unending hunger for purpose and belonging . . .

I've got degrees they say no one can take away, but please take 'em
I'll take usurious loans and sell myself, but not oversell or undersell
Hard skills, soft skills, hardcore, softcore
I'll be anything you want me to be and authentic, too
I'm not desperate, you see
Unless you want me to be

Like your foreign policy, let me boil blood and treasure for a chance
I do everything I know how to do for you in advance
Days on the forms, fists on the floor
And still you want more until I die an inefficient bore
Which is fine, as long as it's for your . . .

Your pearl of great price was given to so many before
And doesn't really exist anymore
If it did, I couldn't cover the bill
And it's truly worthless, still . . .

Still . . .
May I have PURPOSE AND BELONGING?

CONMAN

I'm confident you believe that confidence is supreme
And I'm confident you know that I tire of this theme
I'm confident that you are never going to see
And I'm confident you aren't confident in me

Confidentially I don't see added value for me
To confidentially accuse confidence as empty
Confidentially whys are impotent without hows
To confidently change eternities without changes to nows

TO THE VICTOR GOES THE DARWIN AWARD

There are two men.

One is the man I wish to be.

The other is the man I wish not to be.

Today, the latter went about the same old crap and fills his
opportunity to write with vanity.

The former was dragged from the keyboard and stuffed in a box.

He was a better man.

He did not win.

Where were you on that one, evolution?

YOU KNOW THE DRILL, I KNOW THE BIT

You know the drill, I know the bit
Too many places to lie, nowhere to sit
Too few spaces for truth, and less among youth
You know the drill, I know the bit

I know the drill, you know the bit
You went for the screw, but it didn't fit
Your flathead is a knife, it runs flush for life
I know the drill, you know the bit

ON THE GROUND

Let the stones fly, and then sum the amount
I have many sins, being me doesn't count
You're casting aspersions from a rickety tower
View must be nice, and I shouldn't cower
But I do

It's a mess in the mud, I must say
Now I've said it aloud, and that's not okay
The fortress is wide, but not wide enough
For the little I've got, because it's just stuff
But it's new

So I flee to the forest, the best place to be
Away from your aim and safe in a tree
We each bet on hunger for the other to quit
You doubted my gut and thought I'd be it
But it's you

STAYING ON TARGETS

The Japanese say
One who chases two rabbits
Goes home hungry

Fortunately for me
I'm chasing three

Day job for feeding mouth
Night job for feeding soul
This job for feeding soul again

I am so-so at that day job
And less so at that night job
Going more so for this job

So I hope home will still have me
Even if I am still hungry

VI: DISCOURSE DISMISSED

VENTURING FOR VENOM

The path to success is actually the wide and easy one
They don't say that so honest people will take the treacherous path
What kind of treachery awaits honesty, you may ask
You should know if you honestly ask

This road is longer, narrower, steeper, rockier, and darker
With many fake forks that lead to thorns, cliffs, and beasts
The piles of bodies here will make you question if it's worth it
And we haven't even reached the worst part yet

For past the highest peaks when respite is in sight
There descends from the wide path of success
A vine where the cruelest vipers of the successful
Wind and prey upon those who come this way

With scales of steel, they are charged with keeping out the riffraff
They demand ever more proof that you belong among them
And the final trick is that when you provide such proof as asked
Their task is to sink doubt and dismissal in destructive criticism

Trifling writhes in your veins and pettiness never leaves your mind
Subjective as objective critiques will make you regret all honesty
Yet even those among you will tell you that the way out is through
Maybe for them
But a sickly shell fallen into deathly success becomes you

BE (LONGING)

I've always wanted to belong. (Despite my integral independence streak.)

Yet I've always had trouble making friends. (For I'm an oddball with social anxiety.)

I find team sports oddly alluring. (Which I can only take casually, not seriously.)

I've played in many short-lived bands. (Wishing others would take seriously, not casually.)

I made Eagle Scout. (After being denied the Order of the Arrow peer up-down vote . . . twice.)

I accept intense differences of politics and religion. (Except I'm not accepted into an affiliation.)

For my strategic mind and servant leadership, I missed a calling as an armed forces officer. (All four recruiters shuddered at my health history and I'm a peacenik anti-interventionist anyway.)

So I've tried to be a blood brother in nonprofit social services. (That's irony you can taste.)

Program coordinators and clients seem to like me. (Most managers seem to want me to quit.)

As a teacher, professors compliment my methods and students appreciate their applied skills. (Administrators don't.)

And if at first hundredth I don't succeed, I try, try again! (Try thousandth on the job rejections.)

Given how all of that went, I now wish to connect with you. (. . . And how is that going, exactly?)

UNHELPFUL THOUGHTS SERVED DAILY

If you try to do any given task or application, it will take more time and energy than anticipated and wipe out your motivation to do other tasks and applications.

X should be done before y which should be done before z which should be done before x. (You need the money for the car for the job for the money.)

Effort will lead to your symptoms while lack of effort will lead to the underlying problem getting worse.

I told you your motivation was going to be wiped out.

Don't get mad, don't get mad, don't get mad, don't get mad, don't — dammit.

Don't bitch, don't bitch, don't bitch, don't bitch, don't — dammit.

Your preferred coping strategy is sitting on your ass and scrolling your life away.

Don't comment with indisputable evidence because you'll offend people.

Don't get mad, don't get mad, don't get mad, don't get mad, don't —

dammit.

Attempting to communicate means being misunderstood and more discord.

If you wear what you want to wear, people will dislike you. If you wear what you think they want you to wear, people will intuit that you're a fake and will still dislike you. But not as much.

THE FIGHTERS VS. THE CRICKETS

What a beautiful day to stay inside on social media! First off, thank you to our sponsors, the Algorithms and Advertisers. We've got a great game today! This time, it's courtesy of some friendly neighborhood Pissant Poster. Now, we've seen so many close matches over the web between Ideological Inflammation, Call-Out Culture, Precious Pics, and Clever Quips that have all won the Approving Attention Bowl. All year, every year! Nothing like the All-Humanitarian League playing on the Tribal Fields in the greatest stadium of all, the Echo Chamber! All the wild fans come out no matter how predictable the games are. What if we were to shake it up?

Because we have a hell of a matchup ready to respond to that Pissant Poster. For those of you season ticket holders who want something a little different from self-righteous callouts, confirmation bias-laden articles, and showoff derivatives for your entertainment, today's game features . . . evidence-based analysis, NUANCE, critical thinking, and get this: ACTION STEPS! Thoughtful yet practical? With no clear ideological bent, there's no telling what's gonna happen! To top off reason with passion, a halftime show featuring that old act Blood, Sweat, and Tears!

And here come our responding players! Sure enough, it's the FIGHTERS versus the CRICKETS! That's right! You weirdo deep thinkers and feelers know 'em and probably don't love 'em, but . . . you should! The Fighters are here to either only respond to tell you

you're wrong by pure fiat – evidence and reasons are passé, sports fans – or make sure no thoughtful let alone actionable take is without a half-baked critique from left field to readily justify Overton Window-approved and predictable ideological bents on everything. Pick a team, already! Opinion is always blood sport. Discourse? Dismissed!

But wait! The Crickets are changing the game by teaching everyone to be happy by themselves and enjoy their thoughts and passions alone despite social psychology research findings to the contrary! Because if people aren't responding, that must be because your content or ideas just aren't as good as others. Everyone knows attention corresponds to quality! Top billing means top-shelf! And seriously, our entertainment is from Blood, Sweat, and Tears? They can spin that wheel and bless that kid elsewhere. Seriously, Marv. Passion? Pretentious!

So is YOUR honest offering straight from the heart and mind going to be consumed by fire . . . or ice?! Or a tie of lukewarm tolerance? Anything (except meaning, connection, understanding, evolution, advanced questioning, paradigm shifts, achieving shared outcomes, more equitable liberty and livelihood, truth, love, etc.) could happen! What a match! Who's it gonna be? Throw down that post and see if kneejerk disagreement or no response wins! Think for yourself with some soul in the game and you'll be hated or ignored, but never loved!

POWER IS AN IDOL

The Church carries a staff
The State carries a gun
You can walk past any steeple
The State can't be outrun

Spare an old policy dork
From talk of impracticalities
I know the weight of blunt force
And negative externalities

And beware the Mob's fist
Place Law's machete aside
Opt for the scalpel and short bills
Demagoguery won't abide

Ideologies may appease
The tribal sense within our brains
But not shared values or interests
So leave the teams to the games

The only one I wish to fight
Is that old tyrant still number one
The one which says that might makes right
A golden calf with a steel gun

WHAT I WANT

I don't want to dress so damn pastel preppy at work
I want to dress like Latter Day Bowie's residual self-image at work

I don't want to wear some witty new printed t-shirt that suggests a
casual sense of subtle superiority around town
I want to wear some authentic old printed t-shirt that suggests a
casual sense of subtle connection around town

I don't want a nice guitar
I want a guitar that I've spec'd the hell out of

I don't want a nice car
I want a reliable, safe, and affordable car

I don't want a nice house
I want a home

I don't want guarantees by slapping a "right" sticker on everything
I want maximum access and opportunity with no fingers on scales

I don't want self-aggrandizement in my positions on public policy
I want evidence-based analysis on shared public policy outcomes

I don't want illusions
I want realities

WHAT I FEAR

Not disagreement, but discord

Not exertion, but palpitation

Not differences, but disconnection

Not external chaos, but internal chaos

Not discomfort, but panic

Not physical injury, but mental fracture

Not work, but waste

Not unfairness, but anti-fairness

Not obscurity, but irrelevance

Not lack of attention, but lack of meaning

Not pain, but suffering

Not the Other, but the Self

THE UNWRITTEN RULES

We all know the unwritten rules
Those very long drafts about things that don't matter
Those very long roads away from ourselves
Taken more seriously than the most open hearts

For every fashion tip like never buttoning the bottom button
For every inefficient form to be filled like repeating résumé
information
And every scene to be laid in our social realms with nice ribbons
and bows
We scurry past one another

We keep doing it

I can call them out by tongue or key
(Even if this is how most of them live, fittingly)
Yet I am also susceptible to these agendas
And their wicked ends

Perhaps they should be taken as givens
I still refuse to give them most favored narration status
Over the words of our souls, our luminous inner selves
I say let us never forget what all of these unwritten rules are

Pavement with blood seeping out of the sides

VII: CUTTING LINES

KNIGHT OF THE SCREEN

The Grail of Purpose

Searching all of the world's web

Found Two Girls, One Cup

EVERY BODY LIES

Doesn't matter if

I change, anything I wear

Is just a costume

CATIVE LISTENING

You learn some things when

The only one who responds

To you is your cat

WHITE DRESS OR YELLOW PAGES

I don't need a wife

I need a professional

A horse whisperer

THE REAL DECOY

My contents consist

Of Leonard's slouch, Ludwig's glare

Dashed by Patrick's crap

ONE FLAW TO RUIN THEM ALL

One who deals in rants

Is not qualified to do

Anything, really

THE ENEMY OF THE GOOD

Show me someone who

Demands perfection, I'll show

You a hypocrite

GIVE AND TAKE

The goals were quite clear

Ten of this, twenty of that

Gave each, got the boot

THE FINE PRINT

She may well love me

She just doesn't know that I'm

Broken forever

I ASKED DAD FOR DIRECTIONS

The greatest advice

That Dad ever gave me was

To avoid assholes

WHAT GREATNESS ISN'T

Simple, complex, and

Multitudes of qualities

None are quality

SEEING OUR DIFFERENCE

She is effortless

And I am the opposite

Though I have good eyes

VIII: DEAR ALIAE

MY DEEPEST REGRET

My deepest regret
Is not that I didn't major in economics
Or stay another term to get summa cum laude
Nor even that I didn't take that full ride to State

My deepest regret
Is not that I didn't jump in the pool with her
Or continue the fling with that one gal in college
Nor even that I didn't go full lonely hookup with my exes

My deepest regret
Is not that I didn't find my first job closer to home
Or tell that ornery idiotic boss where to place his pointing finger
Nor even that I didn't push harder when the big name considered
publishing me

No
My deepest regret
Is that when the more egregious things outside of my power happen
That my attention goes straight to wailing and gnashing of teeth
Not trying to control the explosion of pitch dark waste anger
spewing between those teeth
Which inexorably lands on you

I am sorry. I am deeply sorry. I don't know how to improve this, but
I will keep trying. You are worth a better version of myself.

PETERSBURG LIVING

There is another life
Where the electron spun the other way
And it was more of a yes than a no you'd say
And we'd rest easy with what we had that day

There is another life
Where I overcame gravity with you
And the oddball feelings would remain anew
And the others would find love for each other, too

There is another life
Where the wet kissing would not end
And all words and things were ours to send
And there would be no misunderstanding to mend

There is another life
Where we had finished what we started
And there was no autumn for the brokenhearted
And the meeting of the minds would not have parted

While there is another life
I am grateful for this one, true
They have their faults, as do you
Though I have more, so be grateful, too

WE'RE STILL THERE

We're still smoking on the balcony
Chatting on the porch there by 11th Street
Waiting to see who we would see
Late at night and drinking coffee

We're still swing dancing on the patio
You're just more graceful than this daddy-o
I said I'd try it out, you know, give it a go
Trying not to think of feelings, you know

We're still hanging out into the night
Clumsily sorting through that late teenage fright
Of who loves who and what it all means, it might
Matter less than what we shared in low light

We're still finishing our last cigarette
Wondering how long this longing would get
And when it was exactly that we'd met
When where is the only thing that's set

TO THE DAUGHTER I NEVER HAD

I don't mean to bother you with sentiments from afar
I only wish that you knew how much it meant
Those days so simple and pure that we spent
Walking you through the neighborhood in late September
Down to the park of a rugged old town, where the other dad was —
Well, only dad, but he thought I was —
Talking about how they grow up so fast
And I smiled, not wanting to correct him as
You swung so high, and played with the other girls
I had thought to myself that these were the best moments
And that they would come and go as I was not a real dad
Pushed out of my mind, as I carried you home
Nestled in my arms, eyes closed, never thought we would know
How much I loved you
As much as mom's on-again fling could, anyhow
I carried you back to her place that day with little to say
And on a laptop screen watched some old anime
We just hung out, almost resembling a family temporarily
When it was time for bed, you demanded a hug and a story
I told of New Mexico bats flying out of caves in big clouds at night
You laughed at how deep their droppings would be and how I tell it
Always so sciency and angelic
Asked for a story or three, I kissed your forehead so you'd sleep
I would do so again, but by now you're almost twenty
Lost in space and time . . . thank you for making my old heart young

HONEYMOONS

When we finally figured out the code to the forest cabin
Shuffling in the dark and cold on that auspicious January night
And your dress came apart, and you promptly fell into bed
Immediately embraced by sleep, while it wouldn't find me for hours
It was good to be with you

When we finished breakfast at the diner the following March
Driving back to the lodge and walking up the hill
And sitting on the bench together to enjoy the mountains
Sunlight and rhododendron blooms around us
It was good to be with you

When we finished our tour of the United Nations that April
Figuring out the routes from the Y to David Gilmour
And he began to play the intro of that one sweet song
I held your hand and smiled big and dorky as I do
It was good to be with you

When we walked from the Jaguar Temple in ancient Tikal
Braving our sedentary bodies in August heat to ascend Temple IV
And we sat upon the Mayan ruins above the Guatemalan jungle
Quietly observing and thinking nothing of hurting, looking toward a
Belizean honey-hued moon at last
It was good to be with you

I know I've always been more sentimental

And those days of the first year were especially lovely and blessed
But not others, as we were surrounded by unrest
And still are, only of different kinds that are there to beset
Please also know, even in the mundane or low

It is still good to be with you.

It is always good to be with you.

A NOTE TO NATALIE

O Natalie! Natalie!
Your mighty heart is felt
Across oceans literal and metaphoric

You are the great teacher of lessons unknown
And one known, the greatest for one of our own
That we are not alone

Bluer than our seas together and apart, eyes strikingly inviting
Gathering hearts to where color erupts in kaleidoscopic
Visions of what could be for you and for me

I regret the clumsy attempt of the tribute
As a penguin regrets he can never dive into a sky
And still feels the warmth of being called a fellow avian from one
soaring like you

These deep waters always await us
We make nonsense of distance when the moment insists
And I thank you, Natalie, for this infinite resistance to the abyss

THE THOUGHT OF YOU IN SLOW TIMES

She had an easy but deliberate way about her
Some hair banded up, some this way and that
Threadbare crew t-shirt with cracked screen print across
Worn thin surrounding her lovely figure and we sat

It billowed a bit over fraying blue jeans
The Chucks had also been through the ringers
Rainbow belt and simple cloth bracelets
Necklaces and several old rings on her fingers

We swayed with the canoe at quarter past two
The smell of warmth in the spring sunshine
It was quiet on the lake, and I wanted to be
Right there with you at that place and time

It was good to talk and even better to not
Popping the bottle tops of rooibos tea
You were gracious in those slow times
As you always knew that I couldn't be

If I try, I can feel that easy breeze
And tattered sheer shirt under fingertips
And hear that soft whistling wind
And see the gentle smile on your lips

YOU DON'T KNOW IT YET (THE GIFTS)

You don't know it yet
You've the most wonderful mother
Who loves you true
And a fair enough father
Who loves you, too

You don't know it yet
They've already given you gifts
She her heart and mind and womb
He contributed in-turn
His height and eagerness to bloom

You don't know it yet
This is a particularly vicious world
So please learn your mom's patient will
And if you can do one more
Dad's defiance of social ill

We will try to give you more
For you're our greatest gift
And I'll reread this when soiled diapers are involved
And all other things
That I don't know yet

IX: CONCERNING ENDINGS

THE STATUE

Grandeur, wisdom, and some bird poop
Are what adorn this stolid mask
This rock is only certain on the stoop
And being still, its only task

I am this thing that sits aloft
Easily ignored by passersby
Difference being, when I'm seen, I'm seen as soft
Not this thing that cannot die

I wish to be as cold as stone
Not lose color nor to crack
For a statue's virtue is that it doesn't groan
As I do when attacked

But we share a coupled vice
Of powerlessness and inaction
No greater than men nor mice
While committing this infraction

We are each avatars
Merits measured by the clock
At least we can return to stars
When there tolls the final tock

SCARLET MAN AND SINGULARITY

Scarlet hands are bound with signs
Scarlet bands across the times
Scarlet sands upon these many
Scarlet man's blood scattering

I am the one I knew that I'd become
The stone cast out never to be reclaimed
Left to the river bottom, deep and hollowed
Carved each day by the passing water's way
And when at last the whirling time had passed
I grew to steel for I could never heal
Returning to the land and taken by the forge
Find all that was left has been engorged

Singularity of fear shall feast upon us all
Singularity, my dear, is why I make this call

Singularity of fear is the darkness of the hour
Singularity, my dear, is why we take the tower

Singularity of fear is surging through my veins
Singularity, my dear, is fought within our brains

PUSHING WATER UPHILL

I would think myself a learned man
If learning hadn't come in spite of my pursuit
I would think myself an accomplished man
If only because I have to wear a suit
Effort toward what end?

Some say there is a way to develop mastery eternal
Yet I've found myself an exception to the 10,000-Hour Rule
Practice can make imperfect, says the academic journal
Finding that it explains little variation of skill renewal
How will the effort end?

We all miss things left behind
Perhaps the one I miss the most
Is my sense of efficacy, however welcomed
Is the guest that I did ghost
Where did my effort end?

Grinding into infinitude
My effort spins with my song of dire
Awaiting chance or impulse or who knows
To either move or to expire
Is this my effort's end?

EVERGREEN ENCOUNTER

Out ahead by the forest edge
Where light gives way to the dark
And underneath the canopy of autumn leaves
In the shade among gnarled trees
The unheard voice of time itself
Is spoken to the land and back
And the foothill ridge is lined with evergreens

Through the figure standing still
Through the same one looking back
Through this individual at birth
The self stands apart to find itself again

There's a smell of leaves on busy roads
And a clarity in the windswept air
Though the encounter is far away
The passing thought has brought me there
I have come bearing an answer, true
With books and blades and honor, too
If you will come and hear what I knew

That there is comfort in the cold
That there is purpose in the trip
That there is company from on high
That there is more within the forest still

After besting all these beasts within
The ever deeper woods beckon
Our adversaries lost to the common sites of daylight
We've turned away the logic of the land
So claws will find our necks with ease
The darkest ones do as they please
Our bloodied eye doubts what it sees

The path back to the victorious sight
The glow of campfire in the air
The camaraderie defying time and space
The solemnity of standing there

WHAT WE REMEMBER (SERGEANT HOWDY)

What I remember
A road trip in September
A bright day diner in December
Always calling clerks by their name
Listening to the rock station down old lanes
Letting me read and watch horror at young ages
Giving to all those blood drives and the fundraisers
Getting guitar tabs and other priorities of the early internet
Talking over Thai, asking them to make it as spicy as it can get
Chatting up the passerby, observations on things
Sparing that one guy who wanted to fight
Watching Tarantino flicks late at night
Laughing about the absurdities of life
Your tuxedo cat Molly still waiting
A last visit, the kid step we discuss
Wanting to leave with us

What you remembered
Not much by then
Old songs
Our faces
And your forward artillery observer call sign calling in coordinates
FIRE FIRE SERGEANT HOWDY FIRE
Whispered to my sister
At the end

WAITING FOR REVELATIONS

There is a light at the end of the tunnel
We just don't know if the tunnel is trouble in life
Or is life itself

The Hanged Man watches the world waiting to combust
It's in the cards 'cuz Neo-Cons conned us into a tanked economy
wherein we must
Give it all every day to try to find a purpose but then again
Division of labor has labored to be relevant when
It falls apart, the sinner cannot hold
To his own sin of self-interest or even do as he is told
The wealth of nations sold to permanent war, the future as collateral
Delete the surplus population how and when without a why for their
Hopes and dreams, education and schemes, ends without means
But the Neo-Cons, you see, saw to these
Saber-rattling with nuclear powers and all the Neo-Libs agreed
Startin' it and talkin' shit with a nuke fit Russian oligarch, see
Freedom's a service of lips
Pestilence sits now on its pale horse, time for a good old-fashioned
APOCALYPSE

I have no reason to be here, so there might as well not be a here
I have no qualm with anyone, only all the qualms with everyone

We're all all connected and have never been so alone
I know I am no better but we all know the whole world has to atone

So we sit at home waiting to be shown how this world will be blown
Or cut to the chase and finally face how outer demons replace our
inner disgrace
So we must embrace the critical considerations on all of these issues
with real grace
And each other . . .
And each other . . .
All one another
Or it's mother! Earth's time to end this motherfucker

That's why I make a list to be a survivalist while being pissed finding
calm in resistance this
Dropping 7.62 in a magazine or two when I want nothing with you
until after the bombs blew
We all knew it's nothing new, no, it's nothing new
Just like sitting at home, no one on the phone, all alone without you
What are we going to do but wait for you to . . .

This mass equation must be solved or it's doomsday for us all
We might start with the fiscal reality under our physical reality, call
LBJ showed the way that guns and butter was disastrous, to say
Nothing of the bodies and bloodied sent home who'd never be okay
Like my father, forever scarred, didn't even need a draft card
Agreed to leave as he believed they'd see victory even if marred
Enlisted Marine, positioned in the piston of global shifting, how far
we've strayed
Drifting for decades until more blood is spilled, patriotism betrayed
Let's cut the crap on Military-Industrial Complex fat cat fiscal trap

We've already lost the humanitarian and economic cost, how's that
Working for anyone
Working for anyone at all
Except for the damn man, y'all

We can't even agree on fundamentals like ending forever wars
meant to change regimes
Forever wars and proxy wars towards the never war coming apart at
the seams

Until it does explode, and until then, lock and load
I'm seeing this scene so clearly from my commode
You are, too, if you're reading this from the safety of your phone
Because I'm phone-y, too, and just as blue as you, prone
To being just another bitch for the rich powers that be who itch
To provide us reasons to divide us, do you even notice the switch
When each story goes inflammatory, fingers pointing not noticing
Fingers pointing back at you, no one wants to think it through
That we'd have something new if only we would think and feel true
Erupting all the old paradigms and assumptions, pretensions and
pride inductions
Our egos all stand in the way of survival and this new –

That's it
That's it, right there

Not trying to be a kumbaya hippie or whatever

Just sayin' pride goeth before a fall into never

Maybe critical thinking and empathetic linking aren't too uncool yet

They may be our last hoorah yet

Because if we don't learn soon

Head downstairs when you hear the kaboom

CONCERNING ENDINGS

You always want to end on a good note
Even if you have to play a little longer

Alas, then, my plans are foiled
My wife deserves a husband
And my child a father

My God a servant

My Devil an enemy

Seriously, fuck him

Rock

ABOUT THE AUTHOR

Patrick Ashe is a writer and rock musician with over a decade of experience in nonprofit program evaluation. He is an Eagle Scout, graduate of Appalachian State and Indiana University, and an instructor at the University of North Carolina at Chapel Hill. After studying and working in five states, he resides with his family in his hometown of Winston-Salem. He is the author of *Upon This Pale Hill* (2020) and *Typical Tragedies: A Book of Poetry* (2020).

patrick.ashe41@gmail.com
https://www.facebook.com/PatrickAshe41
https://twitter.com/PatrickAshe41

Made in the USA
Monee, IL
30 January 2022

90282085R00063